JR. GRAPHIC MYTHS: GREEK HEROES

Lynne Weiss

PowerKiDS
press.
New York

Published in 2014 by The Rosen Publishing Group, Inc.
29 East 21st Street, New York, NY 10010

First Edition

Editor: Joanne Randolph
Book Design: Contentra Technologies
Illustrations: Contentra Technologies

Publisher's Cataloging Data

Weiss, Lynne.
Perseus and Medusa / by Lynne Weiss.
p. cm. — (Jr. graphic myths: Greek heroes)
Includes index.
ISBN 978-1-4777-6232-5 (library binding) — ISBN 978-1-4777-6233-2 (pbk.) — ISBN 978-1-4777-6234-9 (6-pack)
1. Perseus (Greek mythology) — Juvenile literature. 2. Medusa (Greek mythology) — Juvenile literature.
I. Weiss, Lynne, 1952–. II. Title.
BL820.P5 W45 2014
398.2—d23

Manufactured in the United States of America
CPSIA Compliance Information: Batch #W14PK1: For Further Information contact Rosen Publishing, New York, New York at 1-800-237-9932

Contents

Introduction

Greek **myths** are filled with dashing **heroes**, fearsome monsters, scheming gods, and dangerous prophecies. The Ancient Greeks believed that gods and goddesses ruled every part of their lives. Greek gods could look and act like humans, and like humans they experienced jealousy, rage, and happiness. Heroes were bold and fearless, but their **fate** was in the hands of the gods. In this story, a young man fights a monster, becomes a hero, and an **oracle's** prediction about his grandfather's death comes true.

Main Characters

Danaë Mother of Perseus

Zeus Ruler of the gods

Dictys Fisherman who saves Danaë and Perseus

Perseus Son of Danaë and Zeus, ruler of the gods

Medusa Monster who turns all who see her into stone

Andromeda Princess whose parents tried to sacrifice her to a sea monster

PERSEUS AND MEDUSA

THE MESSENGER THOUGHT THE KING HAD FINALLY COME TO HIS SENSES.

KING ACRISIUS TOOK HIS DAUGHTER AND GRANDSON OUT OF THE CHAMBER AND LOCKED THEM IN A **TRUNK**.

THE KING'S SERVANTS DID NOT LIKE IT, BUT THEY DID AS THE KING ORDERED.

ZEUS WASN'T HAPPY TO SEE HIS SON BEING PUT OUT TO SEA IN A LOCKED TRUNK.

I'LL **BATTER** IT JUST ENOUGH SO THAT THE LOCK BREAKS OPEN AND THE TRUNK FALLS APART.

ZEUS MADE SURE THAT WHEN THE TRUNK BROKE APART, DICTYS THE FISHERMAN WAS NEARBY.

THANK YOU FOR SAVING MY BABY AND ME.

I COULD NOT HAVE JUST LET YOU DROWN.

I'VE TOLD THE KING I DON'T WANT TO MARRY HIM. I'M VERY HAPPY WHERE I AM.

THE KING ALWAYS GETS WHAT HE WANTS, MY LADY.

I'LL PROTECT YOU, MOTHER.

THE YEARS WENT BY. WHEN WORD OF HOW BEAUTIFUL DANAË WAS REACHED THE KING OF THE LAND, POLYDECTES, HE ASKED HER TO MARRY HIM AGAIN AND AGAIN.

KING POLYDECTES SENT A GROUP OF SOLDIERS TO CAPTURE DANAË AND BRING HER BACK TO HIM.

HER SON PERSEUS MUST HAVE USED MAGIC. HE FOUGHT US OFF.

PERSEUS HAD A MESSAGE FOR YOU: "MY MOTHER WILL MARRY WHEN AND WHOM SHE PLEASES."

I NEED TO GET RID OF THAT LITTLE TROUBLEMAKER.

FURIOUS, KING POLYDECTES ORDERED HIS MEN TO FIND HIM A NEW BRIDE, AND HE BEGAN TO MAKE WEDDING PLANS.

EVERYONE WAS EXPECTED TO GIVE THE KING AND HIS NEW BRIDE A GIFT.

I WILL CATCH ENOUGH FISH TO FEED THE GUESTS.

I WILL SEND MY BLESSING.

I HAVE NOTHING TO OFFER. I DO NOT KNOW WHAT TO DO.

I WILL GIVE YOU ANYTHING YOU ASK, MY KING.

HOW GENEROUS. HOW ABOUT BRINGING ME THE HEAD OF MEDUSA?

WHAT'S MEDUSA?

PERSEUS WOULD SOON LEARN THAT MEDUSA WAS A HORRIBLE CREATURE, SO HORRIBLE THAT NO ONE WHO HAD SEEN HER HAD LIVED TO TELL THE **TALE**.

THE GODS ATHENA AND HERMES GAVE PERSEUS A SHINING SHIELD AND A POWERFUL SWORD TO HELP HIM SLAY MEDUSA.

WITH THE GODS ON MY SIDE, I KNOW I WILL SUCCEED.

ATHENA TOLD HIM TO LOOK FOR THE GRAEAE SISTERS AND ASK THEM WHERE TO FIND THE **NYMPHS** OF THE WEST.

THE GRAEAE SISTERS HAD ONLY ONE EYE AND ONE TOOTH, WHICH THEY HAD TO SHARE. HOWEVER, THE EYE COULD SEE VERY FAR AND THE TOOTH COULD **DEVOUR** A MAN.

I MUST WAIT UNTIL THEY ARE PASSING THE EYE BACK AND FORTH AND THEY ARE ALL BLIND. THEN I CAN APPROACH THEM.

PERSEUS CREPT TOWARD THE FEARSOME SISTERS AS THEY WERE PASSING THE EYE AND SNATCHED BOTH THE EYE AND THE TOOTH.

PERSEUS REFUSED TO RETURN THE EYE OR THE TOOTH UNTIL THE SISTERS TOLD HIM WHERE TO FIND THE NYMPHS OF THE WEST.

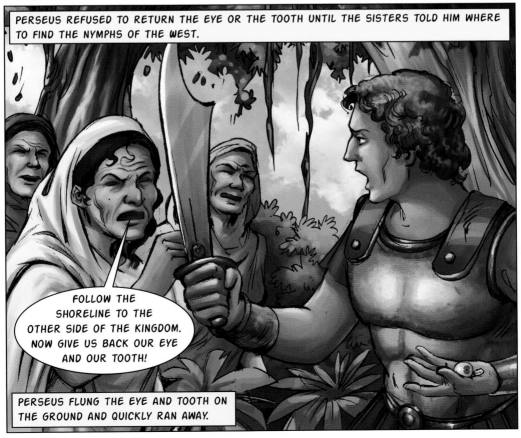

FOLLOW THE SHORELINE TO THE OTHER SIDE OF THE KINGDOM. NOW GIVE US BACK OUR EYE AND OUR TOOTH!

PERSEUS FLUNG THE EYE AND TOOTH ON THE GROUND AND QUICKLY RAN AWAY.

FINALLY, PERSEUS FOUND THE NYMPHS OF THE WEST. THEY WERE AS BEAUTIFUL AND FRIENDLY AS THE GRAEAE SISTERS WERE UGLY AND EVIL.

CAN YOU TELL ME HOW TO FIND MEDUSA?

MEDUSA IS ONE OF THE **GORGONS**. BEWARE! ANYONE WHO LOOKS AT THEM TURNS TO STONE.

THE NYMPHS TOLD PERSEUS WHO MEDUSA WAS AND GAVE HIM GIFTS TO HELP HIM DEFEAT MEDUSA.

THESE SANDALS WILL CARRY YOU TO HER. THIS HELMET WILL MAKE YOU INVISIBLE. THIS BAG WILL CARRY ANYTHING.

REMEMBER, NEVER LOOK DIRECTLY AT MEDUSA OR AT THE OTHER GORGONS!

THE ANSWER CAME TO HIM AS HE SPED TOWARD THE LAND OF THE GORGONS.

BECAUSE THE GORGONS EXPECTED ANYONE WHO ENTERED THEIR REALM TO TURN TO STONE, THEY DID NOT TRY TO FIGHT PERSEUS RIGHT AWAY.

MEDUSA!

13

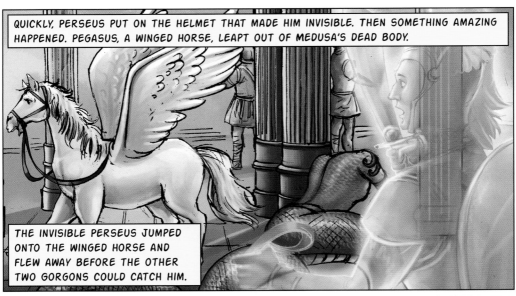

QUICKLY, PERSEUS PUT ON THE HELMET THAT MADE HIM INVISIBLE. THEN SOMETHING AMAZING HAPPENED. PEGASUS, A WINGED HORSE, LEAPT OUT OF MEDUSA'S DEAD BODY.

THE INVISIBLE PERSEUS JUMPED ONTO THE WINGED HORSE AND FLEW AWAY BEFORE THE OTHER TWO GORGONS COULD CATCH HIM.

AS PERSEUS FLEW OVER THE SEA, HE NOTICED A BEAUTIFUL YOUNG WOMAN CHAINED TO A ROCK.

WHO IS THAT? WHO CHAINED HER SO CLOSE TO THE SEA?

MY NAME IS ANDROMEDA. A SEA MONSTER HAS BEEN EATING THE **LIVESTOCK** AND THE PEOPLE IN MY FATHER'S KINGDOM. MY PARENTS CHAINED ME TO A ROCK SO THE SEA MONSTER WOULD EAT ME INSTEAD AND SPARE THE KINGDOM. AGENOR, THE MAN I WAS SUPPOSED TO MARRY, SAID THERE WAS NOTHING HE COULD DO.

THAT'S AWFUL!

PERSEUS ASKED ANDROMEDA IF SHE WOULD MARRY HIM IF HE SAVED HER LIFE.

GLADLY! I WOULD LOVE TO MARRY A HERO.

WHEN THE MONSTER APPROACHED, PERSEUS DROVE HIS MAGIC SWORD INTO THE CREATURE'S THROAT.

AS SOON AS THE COWARDLY AGENOR SAW THAT THE SEA MONSTER WAS DEAD, HE TRIED TO CLAIM ANDROMEDA AS HIS BRIDE.

COVER YOUR EYES, ANDROMEDA!

PERSEUS HELD UP THE HORRIBLE HEAD OF MEDUSA, AND AGENOR AND HIS MEN WERE TURNED TO STONE.

But Perseus didn't have time to tell her the whole story just then.

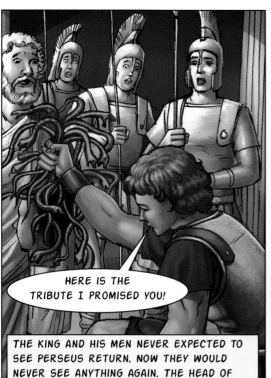

HERE IS THE TRIBUTE I PROMISED YOU!

THE KING AND HIS MEN NEVER EXPECTED TO SEE PERSEUS RETURN. NOW THEY WOULD NEVER SEE ANYTHING AGAIN. THE HEAD OF MEDUSA TURNED THEM ALL TO STONE.

WHEN DANAË AND DICTYS HEARD POLYDECTES WAS DEAD, THEY CAME OUT OF HIDING.

OH, MY DEAR SON. HOW GLAD I AM TO SEE YOU!

I KNEW YOU COULD DO IT, BOY!

PERSEUS INTRODUCED HIS MOTHER TO ANDROMEDA, AND THEY BEGAN TO PLAN THEIR WEDDING.

I DO!

THE PEOPLE CHOSE DICTYS AS THEIR NEXT KING.

HE WAS A WISE AND JUST RULER.

PERSEUS RETURNED ALL THE GIFTS THE GODS HAD GIVEN HIM. MOST IMPORTANT, HE GAVE THE HEAD OF MEDUSA TO ATHENA. IT WAS TOO DANGEROUS FOR HIM TO KEEP.

PERSEUS THOUGHT THAT NOW THAT HE WAS A HERO, HIS GRANDFATHER, KING ACRISIUS, MIGHT BE GLAD TO SEE HIM. HE SAILED FOR ARGOS WITH HIS NEW WIFE AND HIS MOTHER.

I'VE MISSED MY FATHER ALL THESE YEARS. HE WAS SUCH A KIND MAN BEFORE HE WENT TO THE ORACLE.

WHEN KING ACRISIUS HEARD THAT PERSEUS WAS ON HIS WAY TO SEE HIM, HE WAS TERRIFIED.

I CANNOT SEE HIM. NOT AFTER WHAT THE ORACLE TOLD ME! I MUST LEAVE NOW.

AFTER ACRISIUS FLED, THE PEOPLE OF ARGOS WANTED A RULER. PERSEUS WAS KNOWN THROUGHOUT GREECE FOR HIS HEROIC DEEDS, AND THEY CROWNED HIM THEIR KING.

TO OUR NEW KING, PERSEUS!

LONG LIVE PERSEUS!

THE GREEKS LOVED TO COMPETE AND TO WATCH GREAT ATHLETES. THEY OFTEN ASKED PERSEUS TO JOIN IN THE GAMES. ONE YEAR HE WAS INVITED TO COMPETE AT THE **COLISEUM** IN THE CITY OF LARISSA.

KING ACRISIUS, VERY OLD NOW, SAT IN THE STANDS. HE HAD NO IDEA THAT PERSEUS WAS GOING TO THROW THE **DISCUS**.

THE FIRST TIME PERSEUS THREW THE DISCUS, IT FLEW FARTHER THAN ANYONE ELSE HAD THROWN IT, AND THE CROWD WENT WILD.

DID YOU SAY THAT WAS PERSEUS? WHY, HE'S MY GRANDSON!

ACRISIUS WAS IMPRESSED. HIS GRANDSON WAS STRONG, HANDSOME, AND THE PEOPLE LOVED HIM.

BUT THE SECOND TIME PERSEUS THREW THE DISCUS, A GUST OF WIND GRABBED IT AND BLEW IT OFF COURSE.

I WAS SO AFRAID OF THAT BOY, BUT I'VE HAD A GOOD, LONG LIFE AFTER ALL.

THE DISCUS HIT ACRISIUS IN THE HEAD, AND HE DIED, JUST AS THE ORACLE HAD PREDICTED.

PERSEUS WAS HEARTBROKEN OVER THE DEATH OF HIS GRANDFATHER. HE HAD WANTED SO MUCH TO MEET HIM.

I DON'T WANT TO STAY HERE IN ARGOS ANYMORE. I FEEL TOO SAD.

SO PERSEUS AND ANDROMEDA FOUNDED A NEW KINGDOM IN MYCENAE.

MANY GREAT KINGS AND HEROES WERE DESCENDED FROM PERSEUS AND ANDROMEDA.

PERSEUS AND ANDROMEDA LIVED LONG AND HAPPY LIVES. WHEN THEY DIED, ZEUS PUT THEM IN THE SKY AS **CONSTELLATIONS**.

Historical Background and Map

The Journey of Perseus

Many of the places that Perseus travels to in his quest to slay Medusa are fantastic locations full of myth and mystery. As he passes beyond the known region of Greece, he comes to places like the cave of the Graeae, the garden of the Hesperides, and the isle of the Gorgons, which are difficult to place on any conventional map. The ancient myths suggested that these places were in Oceanus, the great river that was said to encircle the world. According to Apollodorus, the Hesperides would probably be located near the Atlas Mountains, the place where the titan Atlas could be found holding up the sky. This would be in modern Tunisia or Algeria. The Roman scholar Pliny the Elder places the isle of the Gorgons even farther from Greece off the western coast of Africa. Pliny also suggests that Aethiopia (unrelated to modern Ethiopia), where Perseus rescues Andromeda, could be the city of Joppa. With those kinds of distances to cover, having a pair of winged sandals and a flying horse would certainly come in handy.

Perseus's Travels

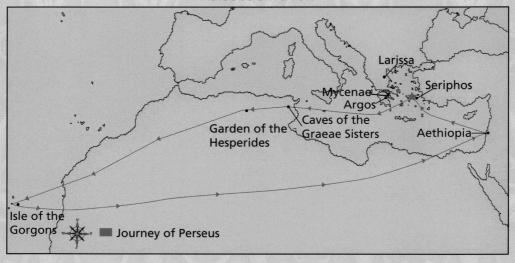

Glossary

batter (BA-ter) To beat repeatedly in order to shatter or to destroy.

coliseum (ko-luh-SEE-um) A large building or stadium used for entertainment or for sports.

constellations (kon-stuh-LAY-shunz) Groups of stars.

descendants (dih-SEN-dents) People who are born of a certain family or group.

devour (dih-VOWR) To eat up hungrily.

discus (DIS-kis) A circular disk that is thrown.

fate (FAYT) The power that supposedly decides what will happen in the future.

Gorgons (GOR-gunz) Three very ugly sisters in Greek mythology. Their hair was made of snakes, and anyone who looked at them was turned to stone.

heroes (HEER-ohz) People who are brave and have noble characters or people who are looked up to by other people.

imprisoned (im-PRIH-zund) Confined or kept in a certain place, like a prison.

livestock (LYV-stok) Farm animals.

myths (MITHZ) Stories that people make up to explain events.

nymphs (NIMFS) Beautiful maidens who lived in the forests, trees, and water in Greek stories.

oracle (AWR-uh-kul) A person who was able to know things that had not happened yet.

tale (TAYL) A story.

trunk (TRUNGK) A large, strong box or chest.

Index

Websites

Due to the changing nature of Internet links, PowerKids Press has developed an online list of websites related to the subject of this book. This site is updated regularly. Please use this link to access the list:

www.powerkidslinks.com/grmy/medusa